Overcoming The Overthinker.

A Collection of Poems on Finding Peace in the Chaos of the Mind.

Raw n Rosy

Contents

ISBN: 978-1-961902-01-5

Prelude

"In the depths of our minds,

we all have our demons,

our fears and doubts,

that hold us captive.

But in the pages of this book,

we will learn to break free,

to embrace the present,

find the courage to grow,

and journey towards peace.

Join us as we uncover the light in the darkness,

and discover the strength within us,

to overcome the overthinker."

Chapter 1:

The Spiral of Overthinking

Poem 1: "The Mind's Whirlwind"

my mind is a hurricane

thoughts swirling like winds

i try to hold on

but the past and the future

mix together

creating a storm within

my mind is a constant tempest

thoughts swirling like a cyclone

i try to navigate them

but the past and the future

mix together

creating a chaotic scene

i am tossed and turned

by the winds of doubt and fear

i reach for the eye of the storm

but it's always just out of reach

i am left with a feeling of vertigo

as i am pulled in every direction

the whirlwind of my mind

never seems to come to a still

I try to hold on

to some sense of control

but it slips through my fingers

like sand in an hourglass

I am caught in a never-ending spiral

of doubt, worry, and fear

A prisoner to my own mind

a constant whirlwind that i can't steer.

Poem 2: "Trapped in My Mind"

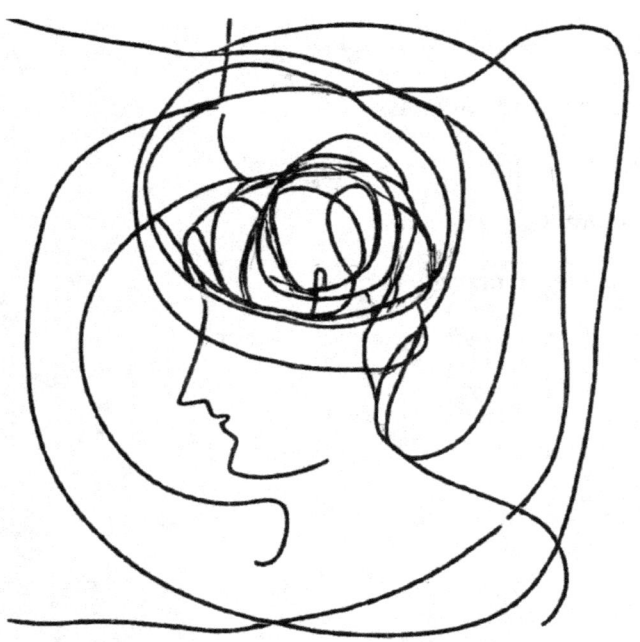

My thoughts are a prison, a cage that I'm in

Trapped by my own mind, a prisoner within

I try to break free, but the bars are too strong

A constant battle, a war that's too long

i am my own captor

prisoner to my thoughts

the bars i've built myself

too afraid to break free

 and live

I am a prisoner to my own thoughts

Trapped in a cage of my own making

The bars are made of worries, doubts, and fears

And they hold me captive, never breaking

I try to break free

But the chains are too strong

I am stuck in a cycle

That goes on and on

I try to find a way out

But the walls are too high

I am trapped in my own mind

And I can't seem to break free and fly

I long for the freedom

To live and let go

But my mind keeps me captive

And I am stuck in this constant flow

I am my own jailer

And my thoughts are my cells

I am trapped in my own mind

And I can't escape its hells.

Poem 3: "The Weight of My Mind"

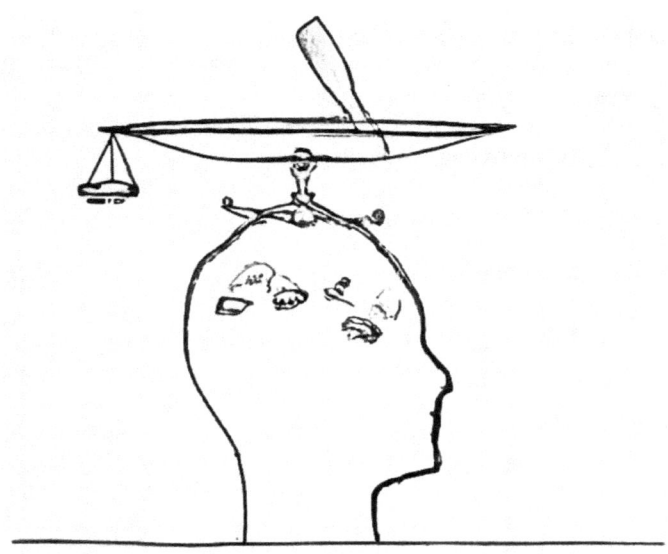

i carry my mind

like a heavy load

it weighs me down

but i cannot let it go

for fear of what i might find

My thoughts are like a heavy load

They weigh me down and make me slow

I try to shake them off and move on

But they cling to me like a second skin

I try to ignore them and keep going

But they are always there, a constant gnawing

They burden me with their constant chatter

And I can't seem to find a way to matter

I try to find a way to lighten the load

But the weight of my mind is always bestowed

It's a constant battle that I cannot win

As the weight of my mind drags me thin

I try to find a way to silence the thoughts

But they are always there, a never-ending onslaught

I am trapped in my own mind

And the weight of it is all I find

It's a constant battle that I must fight

To find a way to let go and take flight

To find peace and release

From the weight of my mind, my inner beast.

Poem 4: "Analysis Paralysis"

i overthink every move

every breath

every word

until i am left

with nothing but a mind

full of what-ifs

and a heart

too afraid to live.

I try to make sense of it all

but the more I analyze, the more confused I become

I am stuck in a loop of self-doubt and indecision

I am paralyzed by the constant need to overthink

I try to find a way out

but the more I try, the more entangled I get

I am trapped in my own mind

and I can't seem to find a way to break free

I long for the simplicity

of just living and being

but my need to overthink

holds me back from seeing

that the answers I seek

are within me all along

I just need to let go of the need to overthink

and trust in my own strength.

Chapter 2: Finding Solace

Poem 1: "Breathing in the Storm"

i am the storm

and the calm within

i am the tears

and the smile on my skin

i am the pain

and the healing within

i am alive

and that is all i need to begin

I am the storm

and the calm within

I am the lightning

and the darkness that it brings

I am the thunder

and the silence that follows

I am the tempest

and the stillness that swallows

I am the wind

that blows through my hair

I am the rain

that falls and doesn't care

I am the hurricane

that rages and destroys

I am the rainbow

that follows and brings joy

I am alive

and that is all I need to begin

To find my way

through the storm and the wind.

I am the one who makes it through

because I am the storm and the calm, too.

I am the storm and the calm within

I am the tears and the smile on my skin

I am the pain and the healing within

I am alive, and that is all I need to begin.

To find my way and to keep going

To find peace, and to keep growing

To find the calm and to keep flowing

To find the strength and to keep glowing.

Poem 2: "The Peace in Letting Go"

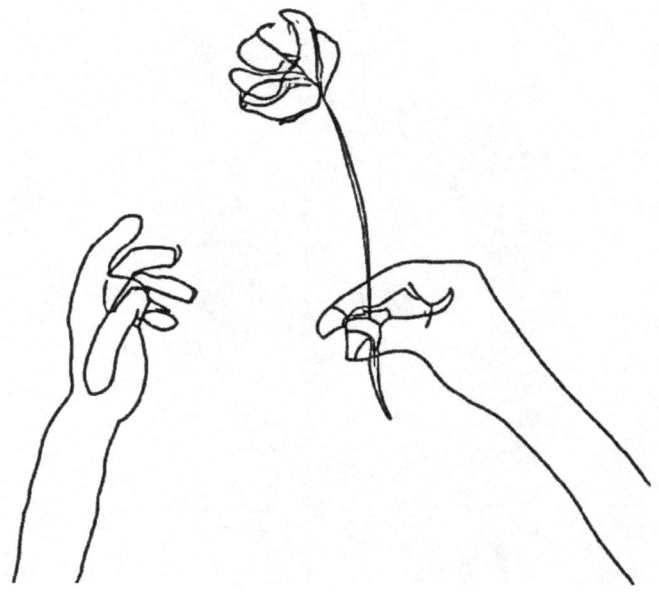

the past is a heavy burden

i carry it with me

but it is time to let it go

and be free

the future is a mystery

i cannot control

but i can trust

and let my worries unfold

The past is a heavy burden

that I carry with me

But it is time to let it go

and be free

The memories, the hurt, the pain

they all weigh me down

but I know that holding on

will only make me drown

So I take a deep breath

and let it all go

I release the past

and let it flow

The future is a mystery

I cannot control

But I can trust

and let my worries unfold

I choose to live in the present

and let the future be

I find peace in letting go

and trust in what is meant to be

The past is gone, the future is not here

and in the present is where I want to be

So I release the past and let it go

and find peace in being free.

I let go of what I cannot change

and find solace in the present range

I let go of regrets and mistakes

and find peace in what it takes

I let go of my fears and doubts

and find solace in what life is about

I let go of the things that held me back

and find peace in the path that's on track.

Poem 3: "The Freedom of Acceptance"

i used to fight

against the current

but now i flow

with the movement

i used to resist

but now i accept

and in doing so

i find freedom in the present

I used to fight

against the current

but now I flow

with the movement

I used to resist

but now I accept

and in doing so

I find freedom in the present

I used to struggle

against the tide

but now I let go

and enjoy the ride

I used to try to change

what I couldn't control

but now I accept

and find peace in the whole

I used to push against

what life had in store

but now I accept

and find freedom in the core

I used to be a slave

to my own mind

but now I accept

and I am free to find

The beauty in the journey

and the peace in the path

I let go of resistance

and find freedom in acceptance.

I let go of the need to be in control

and find freedom in letting go

I let go of the need to be perfect

and find freedom in being authentic

I let go of the need to be someone else

and find freedom in being myself

I let go of the need to be understood

and find freedom in being good

I let go of the need to be right

and find freedom in being bright

I let go of the need to be in charge

and find freedom in being in charge of my own heart.

Poem 4: "The Comfort of Simplicity"

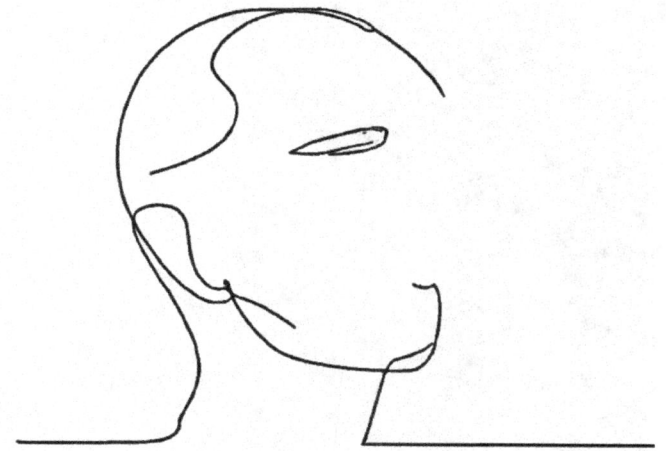

i used to search

for answers in the noise

but now i find peace

in the silence of my voice

i used to strive

for perfection in the chaos

but now i find comfort

in the simplicity of being human.

Overcoming the overthinker

I used to overthink

every move and every word

but now I find solace

in the simplicity of being heard

I used to try to be someone else

but now I find comfort

in just being myself

I used to try to have all the answers

but now I find peace

in not needing to have them all

I used to try to control everything

but now I find freedom

in letting go of it all

I used to strive for perfection

but now I find comfort

in the simplicity of just being me.

I let go of the need to be perfect

and find comfort in the simplicity of being human

I let go of the need to have it all figured out

and find peace in the journey and what it's about

I let go of the need to be someone else

and find comfort in just being myself

I let go of the need to control the outcome

and find freedom in the present and what it brings
about.

Chapter 3:

Embracing Vulnerability

Poem 1: "The Power of Being Broken"

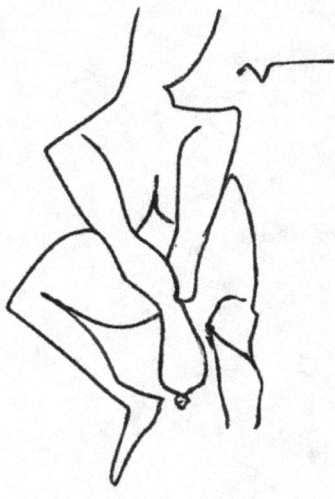

I am not a dam

holding back the flood

I am the river

overflowing with blood

I am not a wall

standing tall and strong

I am the cracks

that let the light in all along

I am not afraid

to be broken and scarred

I am the strength

that comes from being hard

I am not the pieces

that have fallen apart

I am the puzzle

that's coming together at heart

I am not the shattered

but the one who's rebuilding

I am not the weak

but the one who's becoming strong

I am the one who falls

but the one who stands tall

I am not a dam

holding back the flood

I am the river

that finds the way to flood

I am not afraid

to be broken and scarred

I am the strength

that comes from being hard

I am the storm

and the calm within

I am the lightning

and the darkness that it brings

I am the thunder

and the silence that follows

I am the tempest

and the stillness that swallows

I am not just a dam, but the river

Not just a wall, but the cracks that are brighter

Not just the pieces, but the puzzle that's coming together

Not just the shattered, but the one who's becoming better.

Poem 2: "The Beauty in the Wounds"

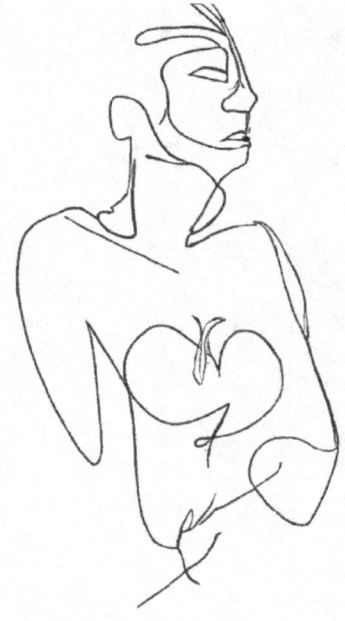

My scars tell a story

of a life fully lived

of battles fought

and love freely given

They are not something to hide

but something to wear with pride

They are the marks of my journey

the road map of my soul

they are the proof

that I have been through it all

They are the evidence

of my strength and resilience

they are the testaments

of my ability to heal and mend

They are the symbols

of the beauty in the struggle

they are the reminder

that I am alive and capable

So I wear my scars

with grace and dignity

for they are the marks

of a life well lived and free

They remind me of my past

and how far I've come

they remind me of the lessons

that I've learned

They remind me of the struggles

that I've overcome

they remind me of the love

that I've won

not something to be ashamed of

but something to be proud

They're the story of my life

and how I've grown loud

They're the evidence of my strength

and how I've stood tall

They're the beauty in the wounds

that make up who I am after all.

Poem 3: "The Freedom in Letting Go"

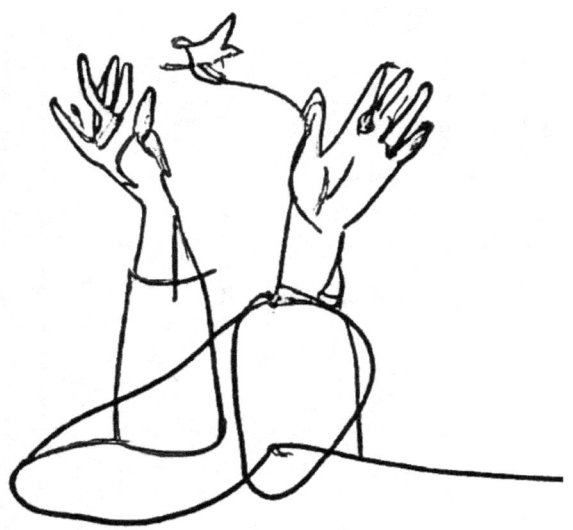

I used to hold on

so tightly to my fears

but now I open my hands

and let them disappear

I used to be chained

to my past mistakes

but now I forgive myself

and break the chains

I used to hold on

to the hurt and the pain

but now I let it go

and find peace again

I used to be trapped

in the cycle of doubt

but now I let go

and find freedom throughout

I used to hold on

to the what-ifs and the maybes

but now I let go

and find certainty in the present

I used to be held back

by the weight of the past

but now I let go

and find the strength to move forward

I used to hold on

to the person I used to be

but now I let go

and find the person I am meant to be

I let go of the things

that were holding me back

I let go of the things

that were causing me pain

I let go of the things

that were causing me strain

I let go of the things

that were clouding my brain

I let go of the things

that were keeping me stuck

I let go of the things

that were holding me down

I let go of the things

that were holding me back

And I found freedom, peace and a new track

.

Poem 4: "The Courage in Being Honest"

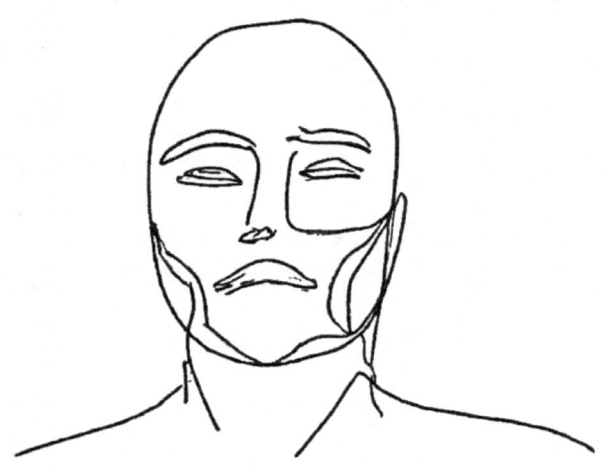

It takes courage

to be vulnerable

to let down our walls

and be truly seen

But it is in these moments

of raw honesty

that we find connection

and true intimacy

It takes courage

to speak our truth

to let go of the masks

and show our youth

But it is in these moments

of vulnerability

that we find the courage

to be who we truly be

It takes courage

to face our fears

to open our hearts

and let love appear

But it is in these moments

of being honest and true

that we find the courage

to live our lives fully

It takes courage

to be who we are

to embrace our flaws

and let our light shine afar

But it is in these moments

of embracing our authenticity

that we find the courage

to live a life true to ourselves

It takes courage

to admit our weaknesses

to reveal our secrets

and face our demons

But it is in these moments

of raw honesty

that we find the courage

to overcome and be free.

Chapter 4:

Moving Forward

Poem 1: "Breaking the Cycle"

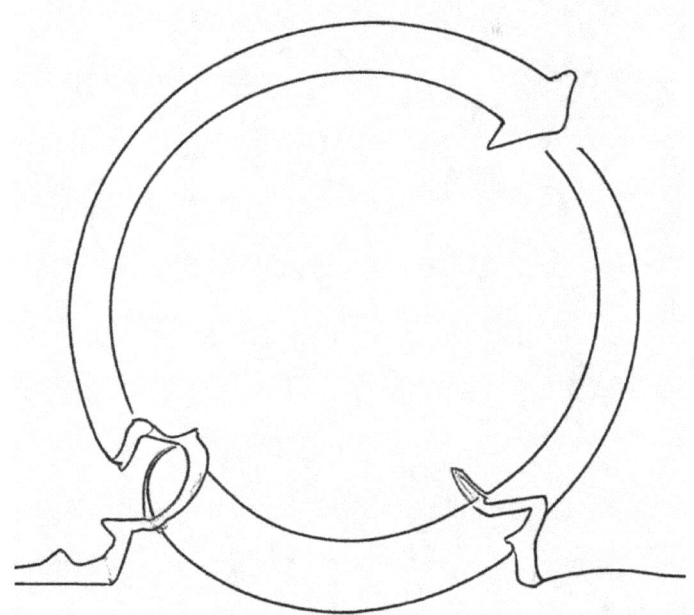

I remember the days

when overthinking consumed me

I couldn't escape

the constant chatter in my head

I was trapped

in a cycle of fear and doubt

but I knew I had to break free

and figure a way out

I began by acknowledging

the negative thoughts

and slowly but surely

I taught

Myself to let go

of the things I couldn't control

and to focus on the present

and what made my heart whole

I learned to trust

in the journey and the unknown

and slowly but surely

I found my way home

....

We've been stuck in this cycle

of overthinking and fear

our minds constantly racing

with doubts and what-ifs dear

But it's time to break free

from this prison in our mind

to stop living in the past

and start being kind

To ourselves and to others

to let go of control

and trust that everything

will work out as it's told

So let's break this cycle

and start living our truth

embracing the present

and finding our proof

That we are strong and capable

of so much more than we know

and together we can break free

from this cycle and grow.

Poem 2: "Embracing the Present"

I used to be stuck

in the past and the future

my mind always racing

with worries and torture

But one day I realized

that the present was slipping away

and I was missing out

on the beauty of today

I made a decision

to live in the moment

to let go of regrets

and find contentment

I learned to appreciate

the small things in life

and found peace

in the present, not the strife

....

We get lost in the future

and trapped in the past

forgetting to live

in the present that we have

We miss out on moments

that we can't get back

and we waste our time

on things we can't track

But it's time to let go

of the things we can't change

and focus on the now

and the life we can arrange

So let's embrace the present

and all that it holds

let's live in the moment

and let our hearts unfold

For it's in the present

where our true selves reside

where we find true happiness

and a sense of pride

Poem 3: "The Courage to Grow"

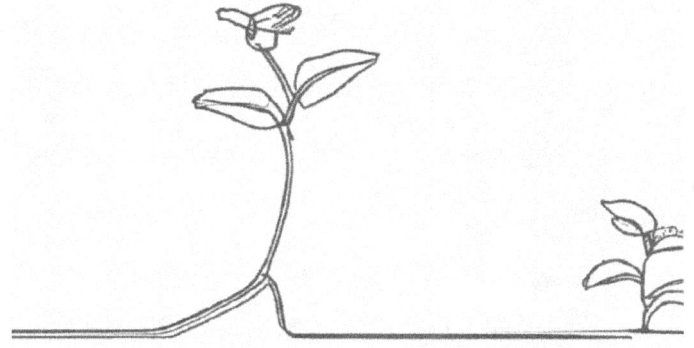

I was scared

of change and the unknown

but I knew in my heart

I needed to grow

I took a leap of faith

and faced my fears

I let go of the past

and dried my tears

I found the courage

to become who I'm meant to be

and let go of the person

I thought I needed to be

It wasn't easy

but it was worth it

for the growth

has made me more fit

....

Growing is hard

it takes courage to change

to let go of the past

and rearrange

But it's worth it

to become who we're meant to be

to shed the old

and set our souls free

It's not easy

to face our fears

but with each step

we conquer what's dear

So let's have the courage

to grow and evolve

for the journey is worth it

and our spirits will solve

The courage to become

who we're meant to be

and live our truth

happily

Poem 4: "The Journey to Peace"

The journey to peace

was a long and winding road

full of self-discovery

and heavy loads

I had to learn

to forgive myself and others

let go of grudges

and find closure

I had to learn

to love myself unconditionally

and accept my flaws

and my maladies

But through it all

I found inner peace

and my soul

finally found release

....

The journey to peace

is not a sprint

it's a marathon

of self-discovery and repent

It's about forgiving

ourselves and others

letting go of grudges

and finding closure

It's about learning

to love ourselves unconditionally

and accepting

our flaws and maladies

It's a journey

that takes time

but with each step

we climb

Towards inner peace

and serenity

where our souls

can finally be free.

Conclusion: "The Light in the Darkness"

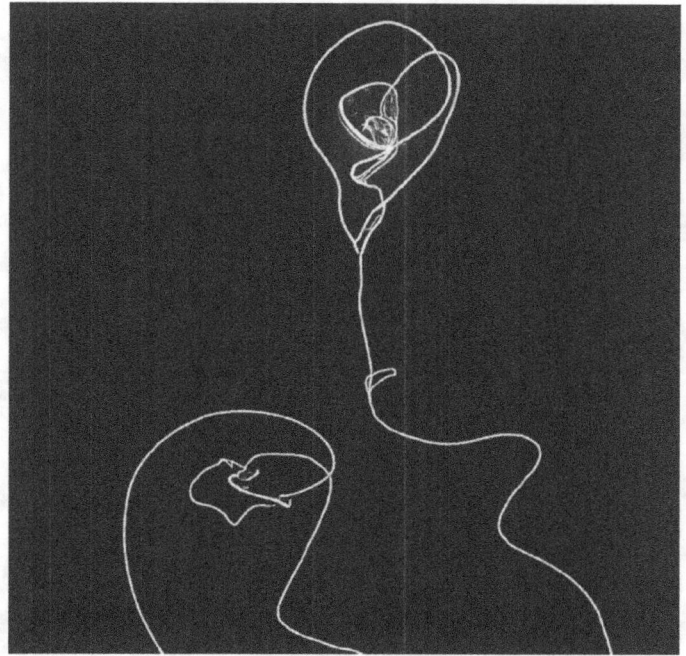

In the darkness

we find the light

in the struggles

we find our might

For it's in the darkest of times

that we learn to shine

and in the struggles

we learn to refine

Our souls and our hearts

to become who we're meant to be

so let's embrace the darkness

and find the light in me

For it's in the journey of overcoming

that we learn to see

the beauty in the darkness

and the strength in you and me

So let's keep moving forward

and continue to break the cycle

embrace the present

and find the courage to grow

And on the journey to peace

we'll find the light in the darkness

and our souls will finally be whole.

About the Book

"Overcoming the Overthinker" is a powerful and transformative poetry collection that will take you on a journey of self-discovery and healing. Written by the award-winning poets "Raw n Rosy", this book delves deep into the struggles of overthinking, and offers readers a chance to confront and overcome their fears and doubts. Each poem is a raw, emotional and evocative exploration of the mind and its complexities. As you read through the pages, you'll find yourself feeling understood, seen and heard in a way that is both comforting and empowering. This book is a must-read for anyone who has ever felt trapped in their own mind, and is looking for a way out. With its captivating and compelling storytelling, "Overcoming the Overthinker" will guide you on a path to inner peace, and remind you that even in the darkest of times, there is always light.

About the Author

Raw n Rosy is a strong and moving new voice in Berlin's poetry scene. The author leads readers on a journey of self-discovery and healing with a voice that is both honest and vulnerable. Their poems are powerful because they are based on real life experiences and feelings that anyone can relate to. The language the author employs is spare but effective, leaving the reader with a strong impression. Anyone seeking to be moved and inspired by Berlin poetry should read "Raw n Rosy," thanks to the author's distinctive voice and style. There is always hope and the possibility of healing, and even in the darkest of times, that message is amply reinforced by their work. Using "Raw n Rosy," one can see the world in a new light and unlock the strength that comes from facing one's own inner truths. In addition to being influenced by the rich and varied culture of Berlin, their work is also a reflection of the city itself.

Recommended Books

It begins with us by Tender Tulip

the ends of Us by Tender Tulip

Never Never never by Tender Tulip

Spare me By Tender Tulip

Things we keep from the light By Raw n Rosy

Regretting Us By Tender Tulip

www.ingramcontent.com/pod-product-compliance
Lightning Source LLC
Chambersburg PA
CBHW071105120626
46546CB00003B/1276